KINGFISHER
An imprint of Larousse plc
Elsley House, 24–30 Great Titchfield Street,
London W1P 7AD

First published by Kingfisher 1994
2 4 6 8 10 9 7 5 3 1

ISBN 1 85697 238 0

Series editor: Sue Nicholson
Editors: Brigid Avison, Hazel Poole
Cover design: Terry Woodley
Design: Ben White Associates
Cover illustrations: Ian Jackson
Ian Jackson's illustrations previously published in
Stepping Stones Small Animals Kingfisher 1988
Illustrations on pp 9, 13 & 20 by Maggie Brand
(Maggie Mundy Agency)
Typeset by SPAN, Lingfield, Surrey
Printed in Great Britain by BPC Paulton Books Limited

Creepy Crawlies

Michael Chinery

Illustrated by Ian Jackson

Kingfisher

Contents

The smallest animals

Worms, centipedes, spiders and flies are just some of the hundreds of creepy crawlies that live around us. Some people call these small creatures minibeasts because many of them are very small and some can look quite scary.

Many creepy crawlies are so tiny that you can only see them...

...through a magnifying glass.

Looking for creepies

You have to look carefully to find creepy crawlies, as some of them hide during the daytime. If they don't hide, these small animals may be caught and then eaten by bigger animals such as birds.

Spider

Spiders can be found amongst leaves and plants. Centipedes look for dark damp places to hide.

Centipede

MAKE A POOTER

A pooter will help you to catch creepy crawlies that are too tiny to pick up with your fingers.

1 Make two holes in the lid of a small plastic container.

2 Tape a small piece of muslin or fine cotton over one end of a bendy straw.

4 Collect creepy crawlies by gently sucking on the straw that has the covered end. Only use the pooter for tiny creatures. Larger ones might get stuck.

3 Push a straw into each hole, and seal the joins with modelling clay.

Remember to be kind to creepy crawlies. To them you are a giant!

Keeping safe

Some small animals have special ways of protecting themselves from larger ones. The baby froghopper makes blobs of froth to hide in.

It is hard to see the leafhopper and the grasshopper because they are green like the grass. The meadow plant-bug is easier to spot, but birds know that it tastes nasty and leave it alone. The bombardier beetle squirts poison at its enemies.

KEY

1 Baby froghopper
2 Leafhopper
3 Grasshopper
4 Meadow plant-bug
5 Ground beetle
6 Bombardier beetle

Pond life

Many insects live near a pond or a stream. Some even spend the whole of their lives in the water. Dragonflies hatch out of eggs laid in water, but leave the pond when fully grown.

Adult dragonfly

When it is fully grown, the dragonfly climbs out of the water. It now has large wings and can fly away from the pond or stream.

MAKE A DRAGONFLY

1 Twist a blown-up balloon into three parts and tie with string. Add several layers of strips of newspaper coated in wallpaper paste.

2 When dry, paint with bright colours.

3 Shape the wings from some thin wire. Cover with tissue paper, and draw on the veins.

4 Cut a ping-pong ball in half to make the eyes.

5 Glue on six pipe-cleaner legs.

Wriggly worms

Earthworms live under the ground, making tunnels by swallowing soil. The worms eat tiny bits of dead plants in the soil. The rest goes through their bodies to make the wormcasts we find on the ground.

Worms often come to the surface on warm, damp nights to look for leaves to eat – they drag them into their tunnels for later. The worms keep the tail ends of their bodies in the tunnels to pull themselves back if there is any danger!

This worm didn't move quickly enough – a bird has caught it!

Busy ants

Ants live in big nests that are called colonies. Their homes are often hard to find as they are usually hidden under the ground. In each nest there is one large queen ant who lays all of the eggs. The other ants are workers. It is their job to build the nest, keep it clean, collect food, and look after the queen and her young.

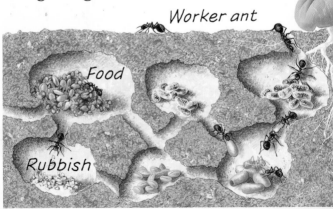

Worker ant

Food

Rubbish

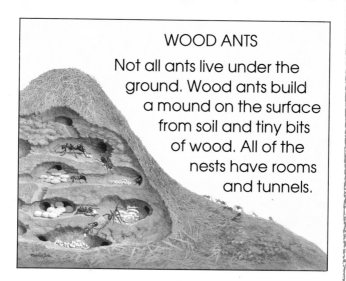

WOOD ANTS

Not all ants live under the ground. Wood ants build a mound on the surface from soil and tiny bits of wood. All of the nests have rooms and tunnels.

The workers look after the eggs and the baby ants, called larvae.

Larvae

Nursery

Eggs

Queen

Bees and wasps

Honeybees live together in hives.
In each hive there is a queen bee
and thousands of workers. Every
day the queen lays hundreds of
eggs in tiny wax pockets called
cells. Worker bees make the cells.

These worker bees are collecting
pollen and nectar from flowers
to make into honey.

The queen bee lays an egg (1). After about three days, the egg hatches (2). Worker bees then feed the larva with pollen and honey for nine days (3). When the larva is fully grown, the workers cover the cell with wax (4). The larva changes into a pupa (5), which turns into a new bee about ten days later (6).

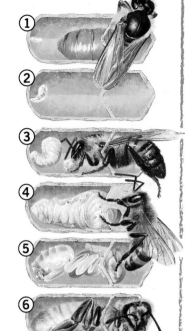

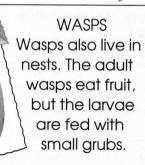

WASPS
Wasps also live in nests. The adult wasps eat fruit, but the larvae are fed with small grubs.

19

Butterflies

A butterfly lays its eggs on leaves.
Each egg then hatches into a
larva, called a caterpillar. The
caterpillar eats the leaves and gets
big and fat. Then the caterpillar
hangs upside down and turns into
a pupa with a stiff, papery case.

BUTTERFLY WINGS

Here's an easy way to make pictures
of symmetrical butterfly wings.

Dip large blobs of
coloured paint on
to one side of a
piece of folded
paper. Close the
clean half down,
smooth it gently,
and carefully
open it out.

Safe inside the pupa, the new butterfly is forming. When it is ready, it breaks out of the pupa and flies away.

6 Flying away

3 Eating

1 Laying an egg

4 Pupa

2 Egg hatching

5 Breaking out

Ladybirds and snails

Ladybirds are small but colourful beetles. You can easily recognize them by the black spots on their front wings. Their bright colour tells birds and other animals that they will be very nasty to eat.

Gardeners like them because the ladybirds and their larvae eat the greenfly that harm plants.

Snails curl up in their shells during the day. They look for food at night. Baby snails hatch from eggs.

1 Laying eggs

2 Eggs hatching

3 Pupa

4 Larva eating greenfly

5 New ladybird

Spiders and webs

Garden spiders spin wheel-shaped webs to trap flies and other flying insects. The webs are made from a very fine, silk thread which the spider pulls out from the back of its body. Some of the thread is coated with glue and is sticky.

The baby spiders hatch out of the egg sac.

Female spiders wrap their eggs in silk.

The spider waits for an insect to come along and get stuck. Then it ties the insect up with more sticky thread to stop it from escaping. The spider doesn't get trapped because it walks on the spokes of the web and these aren't sticky.

Creepies in the home

Lots of creepy crawlies live in your home, too. You may find a large house spider trapped in the bath. And at night you may see or hear a daddy-long-legs buzzing around your room.

Blowflies come into your house to look for food to eat.

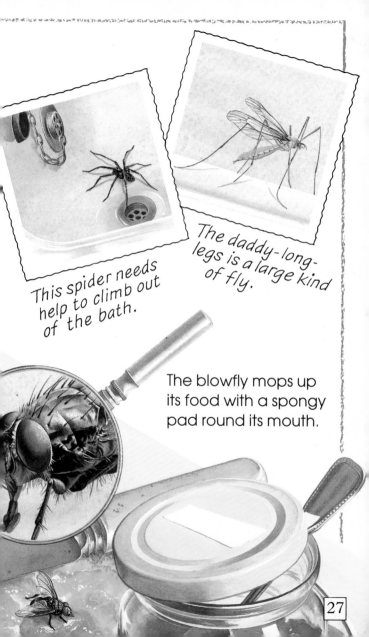

This spider needs help to climb out of the bath.

The daddy-long-legs is a large kind of fly.

The blowfly mops up its food with a spongy pad round its mouth.

Some special words

Insect   A minibeast with six legs, three parts to its body and two feelers, called antennae, on its head. Most insects have wings.

Spiders are often called insects, but this is not correct. They belong to a group of animals called arachnids. These animals have eight legs.

Larva   A name used to describe some baby animals, mainly insects, which look very different to the adults.

Index